Leonardo da Vinci
1452-1519

Leonardo da Vinci (1452-1519) was born in Italy, the son of a gentleman of Florence. He made significant contributions to many different disciplines, including anatomy, botany, geology, astronomy, architecture, paleontology, and cartography.

He is one of the greatest and most influential painters of all time, creating masterpieces such as the *Mona Lisa* and *The Last Supper*. And his imagination led him to create designs for things such as an armored car, scuba gear, a parachute, a revolving bridge, and flying machines. Many of these ideas were so far ahead of their time that they weren't built until centuries later.

He is the original "Renaissance Man" whose genius extended to all five areas of today's STEAM curriculum: Science, Technology, Engineering, the Arts, and Mathematics.

You can find more information on Leonardo da Vinci in *Who Was Leonardo da Vinci?* by Roberta Edwards (Grosset & Dunlap, 2005), *Magic Tree House Fact Tracker: Leonardo da Vinci* by Mary Pope Osborne and Natalie Pope Bryce (Random House, 2009), and *Leonardo da Vinci for Kids: His Life and Ideas* by Janis Herbert (Chicago Review Press, 1998).

LITTLE LEONARDO'S™

MakerLab

BUILDING

Written by
BART KING

Illustrated by
GREG PAPROCKI

GIBBS SMITH
TO ENRICH AND INSPIRE HUMANKIND

To the master book builder,
Bob Cooper.

Manufactured in China in July 2019 by
Crash Paper Co.

First Edition
23 22 21 20 19   5 4 3 2 1

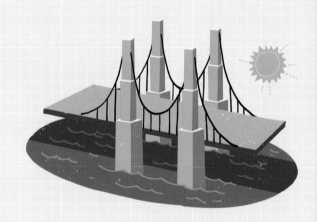

Published by
Gibbs Smith
P.O. Box 667
Layton, Utah 84041

1.800.835.4993 orders
www.gibbs-smith.com

Designed by Renee Bond

Gibbs Smith books are printed on either
recycled, 100% post-consumer waste, FSC-
certified papers or on paper produced from
sustainable PEFC-certified forest/controlled
wood source. Learn more at www.pefc.org.

Library of Congress Control Number:
2018967777
ISBN: 978-1-4236-5248-9

INTRODUCTION

Building is fun! And nobody knows this better than you. That's because building was one of your first activities. You'd set one block on top of another. Then you'd do it again and again, until you had a tower.

Then you would knock it over! There is something satisfying about that, too.

This book is full of building projects. Some are small, some are big. Some don't take long to make. Others have to sit overnight. But all of them can make you feel good about building something by hand. (Besides, building things with your feet is too hard.☺)

Doing these projects will make you an **engineer**. That's someone who uses math and science and technology. An engineer makes things, then tests and fixes them until they work right. That's why engineering is sometimes called an "invisible job." We don't always notice when things work well. But if your shoes are comfortable, thank an engineer. If your phone works, thank an engineer. And if you live in a home that is comfortable, thank an engineer!

When using this book, remember:

- Read through an activity before beginning.

- Gather the supplies you'll need.

- If the activity doesn't work perfectly the first time, try again. (This is called trial-and-error!)

- Always wash your hands when you're done with each activity.

- Have fun.

GET A LOAD OF THIS

Everything that stands has to be able to carry its load. A **load** is a force or a weight. For example, gravity is a natural force. It is invisibly pulling everything down. Gravity is what keeps us from floating away!

Balance is important. If you lose your balance, your load shifts and you might fall over. But if a building does this, it's a disaster! So builders must think carefully. They must consider where the weight of a building is. Then they must figure out what parts of the building will be "**load-bearing**." Walls and posts and columns can help a building carry its load.

What You Need:

⋈ Bathroom scale

What You Should Know:

When you jump and then land, you seem heavier for a second because of the **force** of your landing. Your weight does not really change. Forces are all around us, and buildings have to stand up to them. Different forces include weather, like wind, rain, and snow. Cars crossing a bridge or people jumping inside a building during an exercise class also count as force!

What You Do:

1. Stand on the bathroom scale. How much do you weigh? That's your load.

2. Step off the scale.

3. Now quickly step onto the bathroom scale. Did your weight go higher than your load for a moment?

4. Step off the scale one more time.

5. Now gently hop onto the scale (but don't break it!). How high did your weight go this time? Does that mean your load changed?

EQUILIBRIUM

Whether it's a person or a building, anything that stands needs to keep its **balance**. The word used for something in balance is **equilibrium**. Without equilibrium, things fall over!

What You Need:

- ⊠ Many building blocks of different sizes
- ⊠ A table that's in a place where the blocks can safely fall
- ⊠ A ruler or meter stick
- ⊠ Block of clay (optional)

What You Do:

1. Hang a third of the ruler over the edge of the table.

2. Set a wood block or some clay on the table end of the ruler. (This is to weigh it down.)

3. Place the same amount of weight on the ruler right where it goes off the table. Is the ruler still balanced?

4. Move the weight to the far end of the ruler. Still balanced?

5. Move the weight back to the first spot, right where the ruler goes off the table. Now add some more to it but keep the ruler in balance.

6. Slowly move the weight farther out on the ruler. Where does it lose equilibrium?

7. Continue playing with this idea. These are trial-and-error experiments.

8. When you're ready, move your experiments to the floor.

9. Stand a long block on end. Stack a block crosswise on top of it. How high can you build before your building loses equilibrium?

What You Should Know:

Have you ever seen a cartoon about pirates where someone has to walk the plank? When a **beam** hangs out into the air like that plank, it is called a **cantilever**. A pirate plank needs support on the end inside the pirate ship. That way it balances and keeps its equilibrium.

HOUSE OF CARDS

Building with playing cards is a good way to think about **equilibrium**.

What You Need:

- ⊠ One or more decks of playing cards
- ⊠ A stable, flat surface, like a table with a tablecloth, or a flat carpet
- ⊠ Patience
- ⊠ A room without drafts or breeze

What You Should Know:

Compression is the force of pushing. A house of cards relies on compression to stay up. The cards push on each other and that helps them stay balanced!

What You Do:

1. Be careful. The cards will slip and fall over on wood, so work on a tablecloth or carpet.

2. The ways to build with cards are to carefully lean or stack them. There are three basic card constructions shown. Look at the picture where there are three cards on their sides with a one-card roof. Let's try making that one.

3. Try arranging two cards on their edge in a V shape. Once they are standing, have the third card ready to form the last wall. Okay? Now gently set that fourth card on top as a roof.

4. When you are ready, try another one of the designs. Remember that balance is key.

5. At first, you will only be able to build up to a height of one card. But if you are careful, you can go as high as two cards. (With practice, you might even do three!)

DOME SWEET DOME

A **sphere** is a round shape, like a ball. A **dome** looks like the top half of a ball. A dome can be a very strong shape, because it is supported on all sides. An **arch** is a curved structure that is like a slice of a dome.

What You Need:

- ⊠ An orange or other citrus fruit
- ⊠ A spoon or scoop
- ⊠ A knife
- ⊠ A bowl

What You Do:

1. Cut the orange in half. This gives you two domes.

2. Scoop the fruit out of each half and put it in the bowl. You can eat it later.

3. Cut an arch out of the middle of one dome.

4. Turn the arch so that it is standing up. Take your finger and press down on the top of it. As you do, the arch will squish down and the legs will slide out. That's because the arch has no support directly under it or on its sides.

5. Turn the dome so the flat part is on the table. See how **stable** it is? The dome has good **balance**, or **equilibrium**.

6. Put your finger in the center top of the dome and gently push down. The bottom will probably hold strong. The dome's walls can be squished down, but its shape keeps it together.

7. Your finger will probably tear a hole in the dome's roof before its walls collapse.

COMPRESSION AND TENSION

Compression is the force of pushing. **Tension** is the force of pulling. Experiment with these forces!

What You Need:

- ☐ A friend
- ☐ A grassy or carpeted area (pads or mats are even better)
- ☐ Two or more extra friends (optional)

What You Do:

1. Stand facing your friend. Take a step back. Then take one more small step back!

2. Without leaning, both of you extend your arms to each other. There should be a couple of feet separating your hands.

3. On the count of three, lean in to each other without moving your feet. Let your palms meet and use your arm muscles to keep you in that position.

4. You did it! The force holding you together is compression! In buildings, many arches use compression to keep them in place.

5. (Optional) If you want to see how wide of an arch you can make, have two other friends sit with their backs against the back of your two pairs of your legs. Like before, lean in to your friend and grasp hands. Your arms will be forming an arch.

6. Have your seated friends scoot a little farther away from your legs. You won't fall because you can move your heels backwards to them.

Make a Bridge

1. Stand facing your friend and toe-to-toe.

2. On the count of three, start leaning away from each other. But before you fall back, grab each other's hands! (Seen from the side, the two of you should make a V shape.)

3. You did it again! But this time, you made a bridge. That's because you are using tension to keep from falling. (Many built bridges also use tension.)

4. Carefully let go of each other's hands.

5. (Optional) Have a tug-of-war with someone who is about the same strength and weight as you. By pulling the rope tight and keeping it in place, you are working the same way as a suspension bridge. Maybe you have seen a suspension bridge across a body of water.

What You Should Know:

If a building has too *much* compression, it will collapse. For example, if too much heavy snow builds up on a roof, the weight pushing down can squish the house! And if a bridge has too much tension, it can break like an old rubber band.

THINK ABOUT THIS: Which parts of a playground swing set deal with compression? Which parts deal with tension?

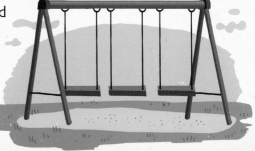

COMPRESSION SESSION

What You Need:

- ☐ Three crackers
- ☐ Three small cubes of cheese
- ☐ A piece of raw spaghetti
- ☐ A straw

What You Should Know:

Concrete is hard and strong. So it is used in the bases of buildings. But, like spaghetti, concrete can crack under tension. To fight the tension, builders use metal poles in the concrete to make it stronger. The metal poles are called **rebar** (short for "reinforced bars"). The rebar helps the concrete fight tension.

THINK ABOUT THIS: Did the Three Little Pigs need to worry about compression or tension with their houses?

What You Do:

1. Stack your cheese cubes and crackers next to each other on a clean table.

2. Using both hands, put a finger down on each stack.

3. Start pressing down on the stacks until they start to come apart. Which food handles **compression** better?

4. Sweep up and eat the remains.

5. Next, stand the straw up on a table. Using your finger like before, gently start pushing down on its end.

6. As you are pushing down on the straw, push the side of it with a finger of your other hand. This will create a weakness in the straw. It will buckle and fold. But the straw will not break.

7. Now do the exact same thing with the spaghetti strand. How far can you push it before it breaks from compression?

CHOPSTICK COMPRESSION

People who are new to chopsticks can find them tricky. Luckily, you can solve their problem with tension.

What You Need:

☒ A clothespin

☒ Wooden chopsticks

What You Should Know:

Using the spring's tension helps you keep **force** on the food you're grabbing. Then you can eat it!

What You Do:

1. A clothespin works by the **tension** of its spring. Gently slide off half of a clothespin. This leaves part of the spring open.

2. Slide a chopstick into the spring's opening.

3. Now slide off the other half of the clothespin.

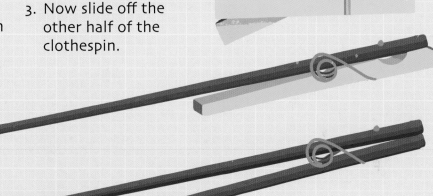

4. Slide the other chopstick end into that part. You now have a pair of chopsticks that anyone can use!

5. (Optional) You can also try this by removing the spring entirely and then forcing the chopsticks into it.

BOOK BUILDING

Some skyscrapers are more than 1,000 feet tall. So why doesn't a skyscraper tip over? Because its **foundation**, or its lowest part, is dug deep into sturdy stone. But what happens if a building's foundation is just dug into the soil? Soil isn't as sturdy as stone. That's where **rebar** comes in. (Remember reading about rebar in the Compression Session activity?)

The foundation carries the weight, or load, of the building, so the foundation is **load-bearing.** With a strong foundation, even a skinny building can be very tall and not tip over! Let's construct a building of books to see how this works.

What You Need:

- Books, at least 10, mix of large and small, thick and thin (these books may fall a short distance)
- 2 to 3 egg cartons
- Lots of scratch paper and or newspaper

What You Do:

1. Scrunch up your paper into balls about the same size as each other.
2. Make a platform of these balls that is at least as big as your biggest book.
3. Now gently set your biggest book on the paper.
4. Continue gently stacking more books on that big book.
5. How high can you go before your book skyscraper has foundation trouble?
6. If you have any empty egg cartons around, try building your book tower again. But this time, put down the egg cartons first, then your biggest book. Did that change anything?

FUN FACT: The Empire State Building has a long pole at the top that adds 200 feet to the building's height. The builders said this pole was so blimps could park there. But most people now think the pole was just an excuse to add height. With it, the Empire State was the tallest building in the world for over 35 years. Now other building are taller.

DID YOU KNOW? In the game Jenga, the pieces are cut at a slight angle. In other words, they aren't perfect rectangles. So as you play, the compression of building a tower presses on some pieces and not others. This is why pieces can be pulled out without knocking over the building!

SLINKY EARTHQUAKE

Things that are holding still like to *stay* holding still. This is called **inertia**. Disturbing inertia is how earthquakes can harm or destroy buildings. This is one reason why many large new buildings have shock absorbers in them. Shock absorbers can soften the sliding and shaking from an earthquake. This helps the building hold still again.

What You Need:

⊠ A Slinky

⊠ A small cloth or towel

⊠ A table

What You Should Know:

The word for an earthquake's sliding layers is **shear.**

What You Do:

1. Lay the cloth out in the middle of the table.

2. Set the Slinky on the cloth so it is standing up.

3. Grab the edges of the cloth and slowly pull it about 6 inches toward you. What did the Slinky do?

4. Now pull the edges of the cloth more quickly toward you for about 6 inches. Again, watch the Slinky.

5. Put the cloth back in the center of the table.

6. Finally, pull the cloth pretty fast, all the way to edge of the table. What did the Slinky do?

7. Inertia explains why the top of the Slinky wants to stay in the same place when you pull the cloth. (Inertia also explains why you don't want to get out of bed in the morning!)

What You Can See:

As you pull the Slinky, its top lags behind. So the Slinky bends, then tries to catch up with itself. The same thing happens to a building in an earthquake. When the earth shifts beneath it, walls bend on one side, and then another. A Slinky can pull itself back together, but a building has a harder time.

CATAPULT!

What You Need:

- ☒ 7 popsicle or craft sticks, or more
- ☒ Rubber bands
- ☒ Bottle lid
- ☒ Marshmallows, jelly beans, or other small soft things to throw

What You Do:

1. Stack 5 sticks on top of each other.

2. Wrap a rubber band tightly around each end of the stacked sticks.

3. Stack the other two sticks. Wrap a rubber band around one end.

4. Open the unwrapped end of the two sticks. Gently slide the five wrapped sticks into that hole crosswise. As you slide in the stacked sticks, they should make a cross shape.

5. Push the wrapped sticks in as deep as you can without breaking the rubber band. Once there, wrap a rubber band or two crosswise around all of them, like an X. You want to hold the cross pieces in place.

6. Glue the bottle lid to the other end of the top stick. This is what will hold things that your **catapult** throws.

7. After the glue dries, set a marshmallow in the bottle lid. Use your finger to press down on the end of the stick. Let go!

8. Experiment! What changes can you make to this design? Would more rubber bands make it stronger? What about more than 5 sticks in the cross, or longer sticks?

What You Need to Know:

Because of the crossed popsicle sticks, your catapult has a strong base. This makes it work!

THINK ABOUT THIS: Do you think this project uses **compression** or **tension** or both?

NOT-VERY-ANCIENT PYRAMID

What You Need:

- ⧓ 24 Q-tips
- ⧓ Rubber cement
- ⧓ Wax paper or newspaper or other protective covering
- ⧓ Work surface
- ⧓ Color markers (optional) to give your project color by marking the ends of Q-tips before starting

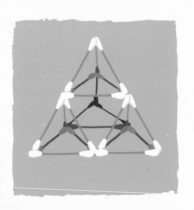

What You Do:

1. Use small dabs of rubber cement to connect three Q-tips into one flat triangle. Let dry.

2. Do step 2 three more times. You should have four flat triangles. Let dry.

3. Take one of your triangles. Carefully rest three Q-tips up on each of its corners. The Q-tip heads should rest together in the center. Remember how careful you were making a house of cards? Be that careful! Use rubber cement to keep them in place. Let dry.

4. You just made a pyramid! A pyramid is a structure with sloping sides that has a point at the top. This is a very strong shape.

5. Repeat step 4 on your other three flat triangles. You now have four pyramids. Let dry.

6. Move three of your pyramids next to each other in a row. The one in the center will need to point the opposite direction from the others. Glue the pyramids together at the bottom. Let dry.

7. Carefully set the base of your fourth pyramid above the other three. Glue them together. Let dry. You just made a big **pyramid**!

EXTRA-GENIUS LEVEL: Try combining triangles and pyramids to make other shapes!

TOWER CONTEST

What You Need:

- ⬦ 30–40 gumdrops or mini marshmallows
- ⬦ Lots of toothpicks (preferably round, and sharp at both ends)
- ⬦ A stable, flat table

What You Do:

1. Get four gumdrops or marshmallows. Connect them with toothpicks to make a square.

2. Then do it again to make a second square.

3. You just built a **cube**!

4. Gently set vertical toothpicks into the four corners of the top of your cube.

5. Now build another square like you did in step 1. Set it on top of those toothpicks.

6. Keep going! How tall can your tower get before it starts to lean?

7. It's time for a new tower with a triangle base.

8. Look carefully at the illustration. See how the design is different? Try to connect your next level like this.

9. But as you build up, look at how you use the toothpicks. Use this design.

10. How far can you go before your triangle tower starts to lean?

What You Should Know:

Triangles are strong, stable shapes. Because they don't get squashed easily, triangles are great for construction.

TURNING THE TABLES

Have you ever seen a stool with one leg? Or a table with two legs? No. These would not stand up! To build furniture that won't fall over, you usually need *three* legs or more.

What You Need:

- ⋈ 20 sheets of newspaper
- ⋈ Masking tape
- ⋈ Markers for decorating your table (optional)
- ⋈ Square piece of cardboard (12 inches a side)

What You Do:

1. Lay down four sheets of newspaper. They should be on top of each other. Start rolling all four sheets from one corner of the stack. Roll diagonally toward the opposite corner. Keep the roll tight! You should not be able to fit your thumb inside the end of your tube. The tighter the roll, the stronger your construction.

2. If you have trouble getting a tight roll, try rolling the newspaper around a broom handle. Then pull the handle out when you're all set.

3. Once you have a long, tight tube, tape the ends of your newspaper in place. Now it can't unroll.

4. Do this four more times until you have five paper tubes that are all the same length.

5. Set aside one tube. Bend it carefully until you've made a tube triangle. Each side should be the same length as the others.

6. Get another tube and also make it a triangle. You now have two triangles and three long tubes!

7. Take one triangle. Tape one end of the three long tubes to the three different points of the triangle. You now have the base (or top) of your table with three posts coming off of it!

8. Now tape the other triangle to the other end of the three legs.

9. If you want to decorate your table, now is the time. Use markers to decorate your cardboard and your newspaper tubes.

10. Once things look the way you want, tape the cardboard to one of the triangle bases. It will be easier working on the floor or a table.

11. Now stand your creation up, with the cardboard on top. You just turned the table!

GIANT FORTRESS OF TRUSSES

As you know, triangles are good shapes to use for building things. If you connect triangles together, you can get a **truss**. Trusses can be seen holding up roofs and bridges. Or forts!

What You Need:

⋈ Lots of sheets of newspaper

⋈ Scotch tape

⋈ 1 to 3 blankets or sheets

⋈ Cushions from the sofa or chairs

What You Do:

1. Lay down three or more sheets of newspaper. Start at one corner and roll as tight as you can. Make a lot of these. Thirty are not too many!

2. You will make BIG triangles with your tubes. That way you can build something big enough for you to be inside.

3. After making a tube, don't bend it as you did to make a triangle table. Instead, tape the ends of one roll to the ends of two other tubes.

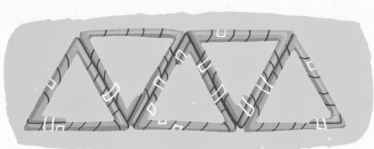

4. Then tape the corners of the other two tubes together. Add enough tape to make a sturdy triangle.

5. Keep making triangles! You need at least five, but ten would be even better.

6. If you want bigger triangles, start with a sheet of newspaper folded in the center. Roll about half of it up. Then lay another folded sheet of newspaper into the unrolled portion. Keep rolling the two double sheets as tight as you can. When you're halfway through the second sheet, add a third folded newspaper sheet to your roll.

7. For big triangles, you may want to bend or cut off the ends to keep them strong.

8. You are ready to create a truss! Look at the pictures. If you made identical triangles, they may slip together perfectly. Use tape to keep them together. If not, trim or bend the end of a triangle before trying to slip it inside the other to connect them.

9. Your trusses can form fortress walls. Help them stay up with cushions and pillows.

10. Optional: Use bedsheets or sheets of newspaper to cover your triangle walls.

11. Experiment with your triangles, cushions, and blankets to make the best living room fort ever!

What You Should Know:

Walls are good for keeping a house cool or warm. That's why they have **insulation** inside them. Insulation is material that helps keep the heat indoors. Foam and **cellulose** plant fibers are often used for insulation. In a very cold place, ice can even be a good insulation! In the arctic, pockets of air in ice can help keep an igloo warm inside.

BRIDGES AND ARCHES

A bridge supports a road over some obstacle, like a stream. A bridge has to "hang in the air." So it is designed to flex or sway a little in wind or harsh weather.

What You Need:

- 2 large blocks, or 2 thick hardcover books that are about the same size

- 10 sheets of regular printer paper (8½ by 11 inches) or thicker paper

- A ruler

- Scissors

- Scotch tape

- Small items like paper clips, LEGO figures, small action figures, or model cars

What You Do:

1. Set your two blocks or books about six inches apart on a table or the floor.

2. Lay a piece of paper over their tops. You have a **bridge**! Try to set a paper clip on it. Now try an action figure. Is the paper a strong bridge?

3. Next, try making a bridge with a beam. A **beam** is a long, skinny thing usually made of wood or steel that is used for support.

4. Cut two pieces of paper in half lengthwise. This will give you four pieces of paper.

5. Look at the picture. You want to roll and tape two of those pieces to make beams. These beams will have round ends. After you roll the paper, tape the ends so they don't come unrolled. Now make more beams with the other two half pieces of paper. Depending on your beam size, you may need more than four. If so, make more! (In the picture, we use five.)

6. Set these four beams over the two blocks (or books). Set a piece of paper flat on top of those. Now you have a bridge supported by beams! Add some of your small items. Hold the flat sheet to keep the items steady. How many items can your beam hold? Write down what you put on it or take a picture.

7. Cut two pieces of paper in half lengthwise. Look at the picture. This time, you want to fold and tape four triangular beams.

8. Do the same thing as you did in step 5. Set these beams between the blocks (or books) and use a piece of paper on top. Start setting the same items on this as you did in step 6. Are the triangle beams as strong as the round beams? Stronger?

9. Finally, you will make folded beams. Look at the picture. Then cut two pieces of paper lengthwise. Give these pieces alternating folds, back and forth. This makes a triangle pattern. These beams look a little like a hand fan. How does this design do under the weight you used before?

10. See if you can move the blocks (or books) farther apart. That means more of your bridge is "in the air." Does your bridge still work?

11. This last bridge is the easiest to make! Just arch a piece of paper between the blocks. Try setting small objects on it. Now move the blocks a little farther apart so that you can set a flat piece of paper across the top. How does its strength compare to the arched piece of paper?

What You Should Know:

Builders are very interested in **load capacity**. This is the limit of how much weight a building, or bridge, can hold without stressing or breaking.

THINK ABOUT THIS: Is there a cardboard box in your house? If so, look at the edges of its lid. Does it have little folds inside of it? This accordion shape like you used in step 8 is a very strong design!

COVERED BRIDGE

Below are instructions for making *one* truss. But to finish the activity, you will need to make *two* trusses. You can make these trusses one at a time. Or you can double the directions in each step of the instructions as you go along.

What You Need:

- ☒ About 50 craft sticks or popsicle sticks
- ☒ Glue (wood glue if possible)
- ☒ Some big blocks, or large books, or even bricks
- ☒ A level work surface (table or floor)
- ☒ Masking tape
- ☒ Patience!

What You Do:

1. Lay out three sticks in a row, end to end, for each of the trusses you are building.

2. Below that, lay out four sticks in a row. Make sure the top row is centered over the lower row.

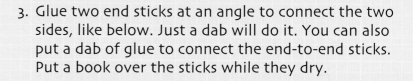

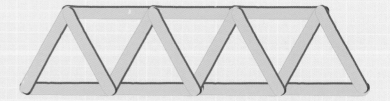

3. Glue two end sticks at an angle to connect the two sides, like below. Just a dab will do it. You can also put a dab of glue to connect the end-to-end sticks. Put a book over the sticks while they dry.

4. As you work, use masking tape to strengthen bridge pieces and help sticks stay in place while drying.

5. After your shape dries, flip it over. If your end-to-end sticks come undone, no problem. Just move the sticks back to the right spots.

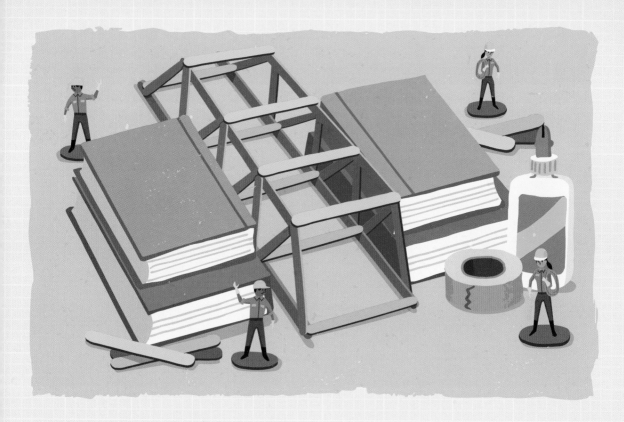

6. Look at the picture. Next, you will glue six sticks in the middle to make these triangles. That is a truss!

7. If you didn't already double this recipe, make a second truss the same way. Wait until both trusses are dry.

8. Prop up your two trusses, long side down. They should be about one popsicle stick length apart. Make sure they are straight!

9. Glue 4 stick beams across the top of the bridge, as shown. Let dry.

10. Next, carefully glue 5 sticks across the bottom. Let dry.

11. Cut a cardboard roof large enough to cover the top of your bridge. Now you have a **covered bridge**!

TRY THIS: If you have a lot of extra sticks, you can also glue sticks to the outside of the trusses to turn them into solid walls.

EXTRA-GENIUS ACTIVITY: If you have a backyard, create a river and set your bridge across it!

DRAWBRIDGE

A drawbridge can be raised or lowered. This is a good way to keep enemies out of your project!

What You Need:

- Roll of string
- Hole punch
- Scissors
- Empty cereal box (or other cardboard box)
- (Optional) a flat rock or small heavy book

What You Do:

1. Use your scissors to cut the flap off your box's top.
2. Punch two holes near the back corners of the box.
3. Punch two more holes near the front corners of the box.
4. Cut carefully down the sides of the front of the box. Fold its crease at the bottom a few times. This will let your drawbridge raise and lower easily.
5. Lower the drawbridge and lay it flat.
6. Keeping the string on its roll, thread the string through one of the holes in the box back.

7. Now feed enough string through to reach the front hole on the same side.

8. Pull the string through and across to the other hole on the front of the box.

9. Now pull that string all the way back to the other back hole in the box.

10. Feed enough string through so that you can raise and lower the drawbridge by pulling the string behind the box.

11. Make sure you have enough string coming out the back of the box. Then cut it and tie the two ends to something big enough not to get pulled through the cereal box holes.

12. If the box wants to tip over, weigh it down with your flat stone or book. Or you can glue it down by using it for the entrance to the next project!

GENIUS LEVEL: Use cardboard tubes, sugar cubes, and boxes to build an entire castle. Or use your new drawbridge as the entrance for the next activity!

DID YOU KNOW? A castle is a home that is meant to protect people against invasion. A fort is a place for soldiers to be stationed. But both castles and forts are usually built on high ground. (Or in the case of a tree fort, a high tree!)

ARCHED BRIDGE

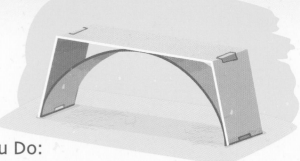

What You Need:

- Poster board
- Scissors
- Tape
- Pen
- Small items like small action figures or model cars
- 2 large blocks or 2 thick hardcover books of the same height

What You Do:

1. Cut one strip of poster board that is 2 inches across and 14 inches long. In builder's terms, that's called 2" X 14". Label that the **arch**.

2. Cut one strip of poster board that is 2 inches across and 11 inches long, or 2" X 11". Label it the **deck**.

3. Cut two strips of poster board that are 2 inches by 4 inches, or 2" X 4". Label them each as a **pier**.

4. Tape the center of the arch to the center of the deck. Just tape the middle part, not the whole thing! Since the arch strip is longer, it will stick out at both ends.

5. Now tape a pier between the ends of the arch and deck on both ends. Doing this will make your arch bend, like in the photo.

6. Carefully move your blocks or books against your bridge, one on each end.

7. Test how strong your bridge is. Can it support your cars and action figures?

8. Check the illustration. Now try adding two or three support struts to your bridge on each end. Do this by taping short pieces of poster board between the arch and deck.

9. Test your bridge again by putting items on it. How much stronger is your bridge now?

DID YOU KNOW? When the Brooklyn Bridge opened in 1883, some people worried whether it was strong enough. So, the builders had 21 elephants cross the bridge. After that, everyone decided it was safe!

FOUND CITY

It's time to have fun building with stuff you find around the house. To get started, look inside and outside for recyclables and other objects that could be useful in an imaginary city or building. Get creative!

What You Need:

- Indoors stuff: plastic bottles, milk cartons, egg cartons, boxes, oatmeal containers, popsicle sticks, paper cups, etc.

- Outdoors stuff: twigs, branches, rocks, pinecones, etc.

- Big, flat wood board or big, flat cardboard surface

- Glue or rubber cement

- Stapler

- Masking and/or Scotch tape

- Scissors

- Markers

- Low-heat glue gun (optional)

What You Do:

1. Your goal is to use your objects to build a city that's one-of-a-kind! If possible, start this project on a flat piece of wood or cardboard. (That way, you don't have to dig foundations.)

2. Look over your materials. What can you combine and make? Can you build something tall without it falling over? Can you make something that's never been built before? For example, if you have pinecones, is it possible to make a pinecone building? If you have lots of cardboard boxes, try building a whole city block's worth of different-looking and different-height skyscrapers. If you have popsicle sticks, make the longest bridge you can that doesn't collapse.

3. A low-heat glue gun is perfect for this kind of construction. It is not too hot, but still, use it only with adult supervision!

What You Need to Know:

Look at the closest wall. Inside of that wall there are probably posts. These posts hold up the ceiling and roof. In a house, posts are often wood. In a skyscraper, they are metal.

MAPS AND GRIDS

A map is a small drawing of something much, much larger, such as a city. A map is handy to carry around or spread out on the floor. Maps are also good for playing games like Dungeons & Dragons. D&D game maps are drawn on a **grid**, like graph paper. Builders also use grid maps to plan projects.

What You Should Know:

A builder's grid shows a large building drawn **to scale**. This means the size relationships between the actual building and how it looks on paper are the same. If your grid is four squares to a foot, then for one foot measured on your wall, you will draw a line on the grid that is four squares long. You would write on your grid paper, 4 squares = 1 foot.

What You Need:

- ⊠ Graph paper (if you don't have any, Google "printable graph paper" and print it)

- ⊠ Pencil

- ⊠ Eraser

- ⊠ Ruler

- ⊠ Clipboard or a desk to work at

- ⊠ Tape measure

What You Do:

1. Go into your room and measure how many feet long each wall is. Write these measurements on a piece of paper. Keep track of which wall each measurement is for.

2. Your room probably has four walls in the shape of a square or rectangle. Decide how you want to turn, or orient, your graph paper for your map. If your room is a rectangle, you may want to turn your paper lengthwise.

3. Decide how many grids, or squares, on your paper will equal one foot. (Hint: If you choose one square to equal one foot, your map will be tiny!) Try to size the grid drawing of your room to use most of the piece of paper.

4. Leave a margin around the edges of your paper.

5. Using your ruler, lightly draw a line for one of your walls. Double-check. Is that the correct length?

6. Using your measurements, draw the other walls of the room.

7. Now sketch in some of the room's big features. Your bed, a window, and the closet are examples. It's important to

show their size correctly, so measure them with the ruler!

8. Label everything on your map. How does it look?

TRY THIS: There are four directions: north, south, east, and west. Can you add these directions to your map? In the future, try to make your map so that north is always at the top.

EXTRA-GENIUS ACTIVITY: If you have a backyard, try mapping it!

GLOSSARY

ARCH: A curved structure that looks like an upside-down U.

BALANCE: The ability to stand without falling or leaning.

BEAM: A long, sideways part of a building. Beams usually carry loads.

BRIDGE: A structure that goes across an obstacle, like a river or canyon.

CANTILEVER: A beam that doesn't have a support at one end.

CATAPULT: A machine that works like a slingshot.

CELLULOSE: Plant fiber.

COLLAPSE: To fall down.

COMPRESSION: Squishing or flattening.

CUBE: A square that has six sides, like a six-sided die.

DECK: A flat platform.

DOME: A round structure that looks like the top half of a ball.

ENGINEER: A person who uses science, math, and technology.

EQUILIBRIUM: Balance.

FORCE: Energy that can push or pull.

FOUNDATION: The lowest part of a building. A foundation is load-bearing, and often underground.

FRAME: A hard structure that forms a wall.

INERTIA: The word we use for how things that aren't moving tend to stay put.

INSULATION: Material inside a wall that helps balance the indoor temperature.

LOAD: A force or weight. For example, a "load-bearing" is a wall that is holding up weight.

PIER: A structure that supports a bridge.

REBAR: A metal rod in concrete that make the concrete stronger.

PYRAMID: A structure with triangular sides that meet at the top.

SCALE: A system for showing how big something is in real life.

SHEAR: The sliding force of an earthquake that slips parts of a building in different directions.

SKYSCRAPER: A very tall building.

SPHERE: A round object, like a ball.

STABLE: Set in place. Not likely to fall over.

STRUCTURE: A building.

TENSION: The force of stretching or pulling.

TORSION: A force that turns or twists something.

TRIAL-AND-ERROR: Trying one thing and then another to see what works.

TRUSS: A frame that helps support a building.